Who Knew...
Baker Flew!?

Written by **Marty Kinrose**

Illustrated by **Nancy Talley**

Author's Note

THANK YOU, to all my family and friends who offered
their help and encouragement. I especially want to thank
Nancy Talley, for your wonderful illustrations.
-Marty

Follow us on Instagram @whoknew_bakerflew
for an inside look at the real Baker!

Published by Martin Kinrose

Printed in China

Soy ink
Environmentally friendly paper

Who Knew...Baker Flew!? Second Edition
ISBN 978-1-7370068-0-0

1. JUV002070 Juvenile Fiction/Animals/Dogs
2. JUV019000 Juvenile Fiction/Humorous Stories
3. JUV001000 Juvenile Fiction/Action and Adventure/General

Minute font by Pintassilgo Prints
Book design by Leah Kinrose
Synopsis written by Forrest Dawson

Author's Dedication

I dedicate this book to my loving parents, Simon and Florence; to my siblings, Rosanna and Jeff; to my wife, beautiful Karen, for being with me on this *interesting* journey; to my daughters, Eliza and Leah, whom I adore beyond words; and of course to Baker, the Michael Jordan of dogs.

Illustrator's Dedication

I dedicate this book to my husband John for his support and patience with the hours spent in the studio and on the computer; to Chance and Finn, who entertain and comfort me daily; and to my sweet Olive, who was a better person than I am, even though she was a cat.

My name is Eliza and this is my story about our very special dog, Baker.

From a litter of six puppies,
we had to choose just one.
When the tiniest pup peed on my shoe,
I knew the fun had begun.

Two looked like their mother,

and three looked like their dad.

My favorite looked like neither.
Would leaving make him sad?

Suddenly, he ran to me
and, much to my surprise,
he bit my blouse
and nipped Dad's beard,
then looked into

my eyes.

The puppy was doing the choosing.
His choice was clearly us.
I'll never quite know who rescued who,
but keeping this pup was a must!

I worried about the ride home,
and whether our pup would adapt.
Very quickly I realized,
all he wanted was a lap for his nap.

First up was to find him a name.
We tried

Fido,

Gizmo,

and Laker.

Then it finally came to me.
Our bundle of love is a Baker!

In his early weeks at home,
everything in sight, he chewed.
Shoes, pillows,
hands and feet,
all were viewed
as food.

Baker kept on munching us,
in a playful, loving sort of way,
till one day Mom laid down the law,

"Our Baker must
learn to obey!"

After starting him at doggy school,
there were so many tricks he could do!
He could sit, rollover, even close doors,
but he wouldn't pick up his own poo.

Soon, Baker met all our neighbors.
He made friends with their dogs and cats.

One neighbor claimed he'd sit on their roof.
Now how could he ever do that?

And then the
unexpected
happened,
on a nearby
hiking trail.
We could hardly
believe our eyes!
Are you ready

for a

whale-of-a-tale?
He ran from
hilltop to hilltop.
Then, amazingly,
out of the blue,
he took to
the sky
like a soaring
bird dog!

Who knew... Baker Flew!?

We were stunned by
the wild discovery.
Our Baker-boy actually flies!
We clapped and cheered
and jumped for joy!
Could there be a more thrilling surprise?

That night round the dinner table,
after all the excitement this day,
our dad was looking white as a ghost,
he had something serious to say.

As Dad prepared to speak,
he sighed a heavy sigh.
"Now everyone, I mean **EVERYONE...**

will want to see our Baker fly!"

"No more simple walks in the park.
We'll be followed wherever we go.
If the news gets out about Baker,
soon the whole wide world will know!"

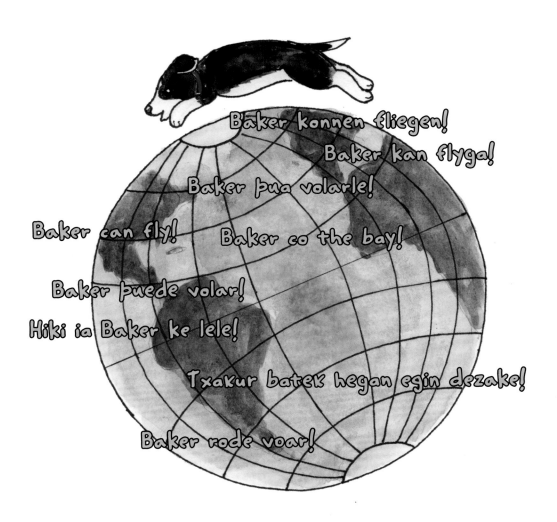

"I've got it!" I said, "We'll teach him a rule:
No flying when others are around.
Then only our family will see him
gliding high up off the ground."

"You're so smart!" said my mother.

"Great idea!" added Dad.

My sister, Leah, even looked relieved,

as we moved from frightened to glad.

He learned the rule quite quickly:

NO FLYING IN FRONT OF OTHERS.

That's right, flying Baker would only be seen

by me, Dad, my sister and Mother.

~

Sometimes our secret was nearly revealed,

like when he rescued that cat from a tree.

Disguised in my slippers,
blue raincoat, and goggles,

they all thought the hero was ME!

And the time on
the Ferris wheel,
no dogs were allowed
on this ride,
so we handed his leash
to a sweet little kid,
said he'd stick by
Baker's side.

Now everyone watched the fireworks,
while the ride took us high in the sky.
Then Baker was with us, and so was the kid!
We didn't expect *them* to drop by.

And so our lives continued,
much the same as all of yours.
Each day was filled with laughter and love,
and a *dog* who helped with our chores.

Baker came with us everywhere.
He watched all our games from the stands.
We'd hear him barking and rooting for us,
Our number one doggy fan.

He was there at our last game of soccer,
against a team much better than us.
With the score tied up, coach yelled, "Time Out!"
And we quieted down to a hush.

We'd lost every game this season.
A tied score would feel like a win.
With a minute to go, we were hopeful.
We had faith in our soccer coach, Kim.

Then Kim put in my sister,
the smallest, by far, on our team!
She placed her in as goalie.
Now we'd *never* achieve our dream.

With just thirty seconds to go,
our fans cheered with all of their might.
Then all-of-a-sudden, I had a sick feeling.
Our Baker was nowhere in sight!

Their team rushed toward our goal.
Their star player kicked the ball up high.
All eyes were on Leah, no way she could block it!
But where was our missing little guy?

You'll never guess
what happened next-
The best play of all-time,
in any game.
Leah rose like a rocket,
blocked their shot!
It was completely
and utterly
insane.

For the first time ever,
we didn't lose,

and Leah had her day as our star!
But all I could think of was *Baker*.
Was he waiting for us at the car?

Then, out of nowhere, he returned!
Where he'd been we hadn't a clue.

Does *anyone* know where Baker went?
Besides us, only YOU knew...
Baker flew.

Dear Readers,

We'd like to take a moment to share a bit about our journey and what we believe is a key part of raising your puppy to be happy, healthy, responsive, confident, calm and adaptable: training! When we first got Baker, he was a HANDFUL, but we knew to start training him right away (at nine weeks old). Sit, stay, rollover and shake were great tricks and a good place to start, but the most important piece of the puzzle for Baker, was socialization. We provided lots of interaction with people of all ages, along with other dogs (cats too!), and made sure to take him places that felt safe and secure. Leash—training, plenty of exercise and interactive play—time were key components as well. It can be stressful — puppies are always cute, but they are not always a "walk in the park." Don't give up. Sticking with your pup and committing to the training process will be worth it, as it's as much about building trust with one another as it is ensuring a well behaved, happy dog.

Pet ownership is a big responsibility, but you don't have to figure it all out on your own. Professional training can be a worthwhile investment, both for you and your dog, especially when navigating more difficult situations, such as older dog adoptions or sensitive rescues. Get familiar with your local Humane Society as they will likely have many resources available, online or in person. Books are also a great tool (one of our favorites is, *The Art of Raising a Puppy* by the Monks of New Skete). Let's commit to raising our furry friends with all the love and support they give to us, endlessly, in return.

With appreciation,
Baker's family

Marty Kinrose is a dedicated dog grandparent who lives in Ventura, CA with his wife Karen. After retiring from a fulfilling career working on behalf of children and adults with disabilities, he took up dog walking and children's book writing. In his debut children's book, *Who Knew...Baker Flew!?* Marty portrays his quirky sense of humor while capturing his love of fatherhood, a reflection of his life and celebration of his family's beloved dog.

Nancy Talley is a lover of animals both big and small. She is a new artist who became inspired to paint portraits of each animal brought into the Humane Society of Ventura County after discovering the joy of watercolor painting. Her ability to capture their unique qualities brought much delight to adopters, leading her to make clever animal cartoon books. One day Nancy was signing these books at a local craft fair (with all proceeds going to the shelter) when she met writer Marty Kinrose and soon began developing her first ever children's book illustrations for *Who Knew...Baker Flew!?* Nancy has enjoyed her time bringing this story to life and is excited it's out in the world bringing smiles to faces and encouraging animal adoption at the same time.